I am a Rhino

Aaron Carr

www.av2books.com

AV² provides enriched content that supplements and complements this book. Weigl's AV² books strive to create inspired learning and engage young minds in a total learning experience.

Your AV² Media Enhanced books come alive with...

Audio
Listen to sections of the book read aloud.

Video
Watch informative video clips.

Embedded Weblinks
Gain additional information for research.

Try This!
Complete activities and hands-on experiments.

Key Words
Study vocabulary, and complete a matching word activity.

Quizzes
Test your knowledge.

Slide Show
View images and captions, and prepare a presentation.

... and much, much more!

Go to **www.av2books.com**, and enter this book's unique code.

BOOK CODE

V972714

AV² **by Weigl** brings you media enhanced books that support active learning.

Published by AV² by Weigl
350 5th Avenue, 59th Floor New York, NY 10118
Website: www.av2books.com   www.weigl.com

Library of Congress Cataloging-in-Publication Data
Carr, Aaron.
 Rhino / Aaron Carr.
    pages cm -- (I am)
 ISBN 978-1-62127-285-4 (hardcover : alk. paper) -- ISBN 978-1-62127-291-5 (softcover : alk. paper)
 1. Rhinoceroses--Juvenile literature. I. Title.
 QL737.U63C366 2013
 599.66'8--dc23
                        2012046234

Printed in the United States of America in North Mankato, Minnesota
1 2 3 4 5 6 7 8 9 0 17 16 15 14 13

032013
WEP300113

Senior Editor: Aaron Carr   Art Director: Terry Paulhus

Weigl acknowledges Getty Images as the primary image supplier for this title.

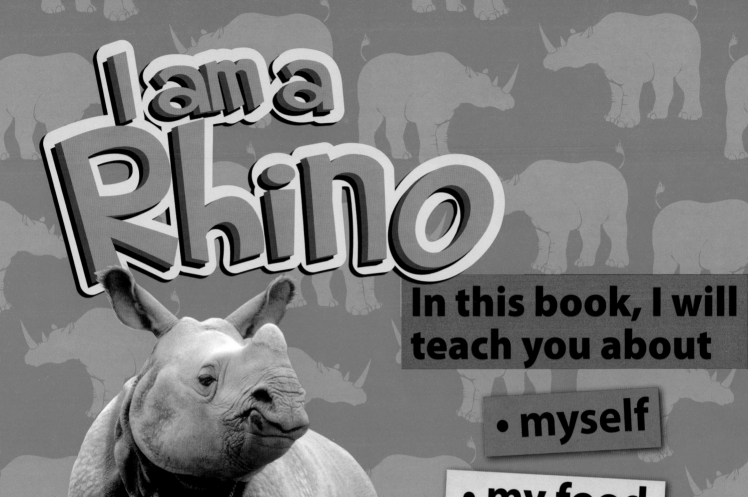

I am a Rhino

In this book, I will teach you about

- myself

- my food

- my home

- my family

and much more!

3

I am a rhino.

5

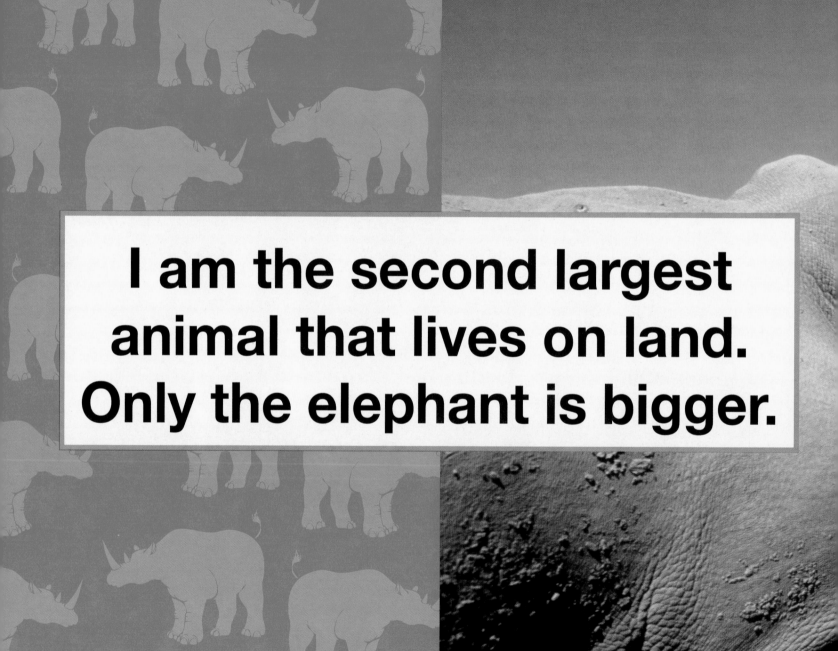

I am the second largest animal that lives on land. Only the elephant is bigger.

I can run
40 miles an hour.

8

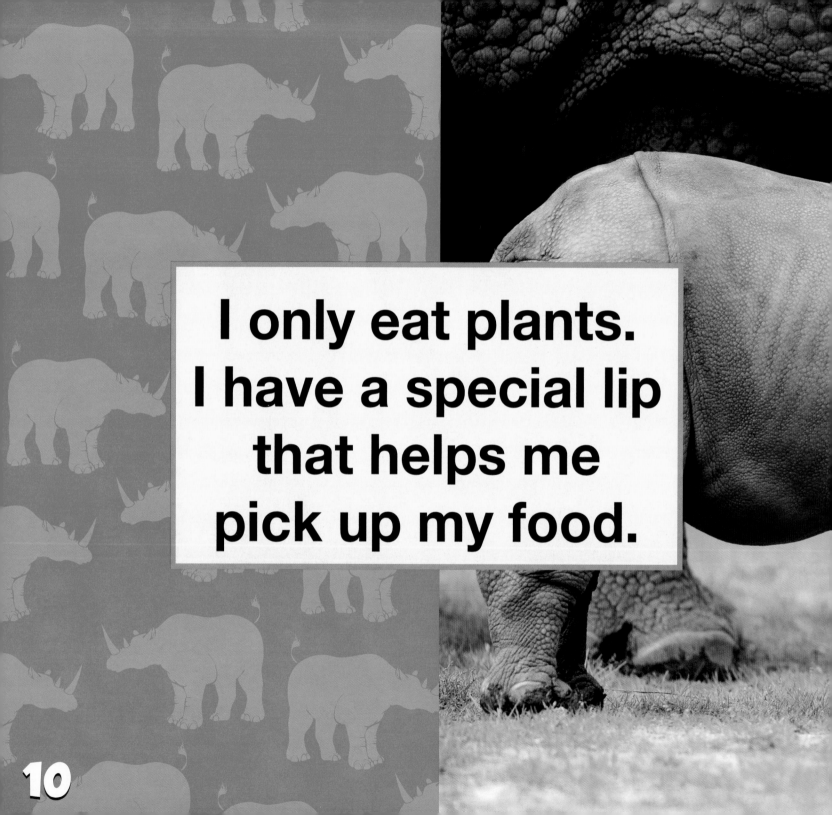

I only eat plants.
I have a special lip
that helps me
pick up my food.

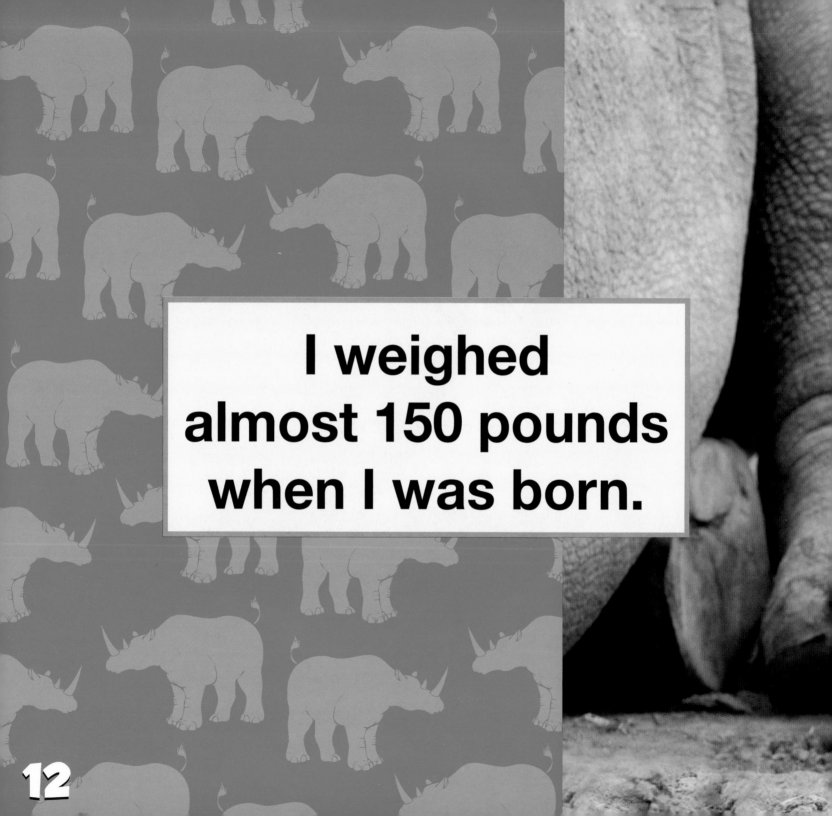

I weighed almost 150 pounds when I was born.

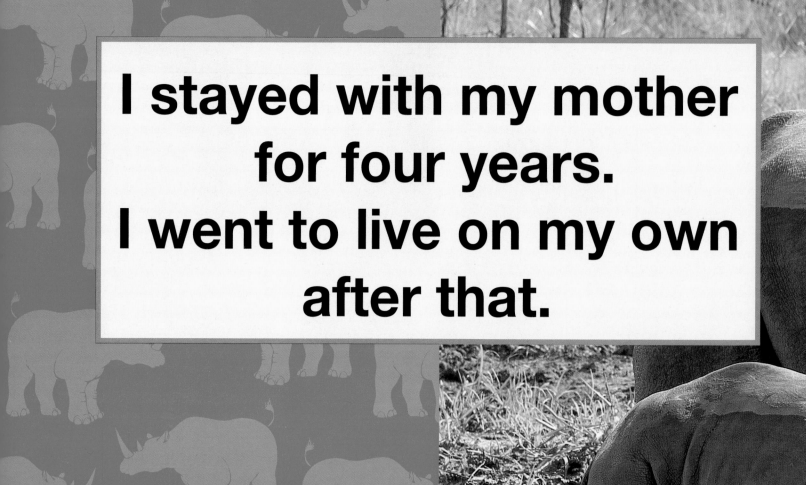

I stayed with my mother for four years. I went to live on my own after that.

I roll in the mud to take a bath.

16

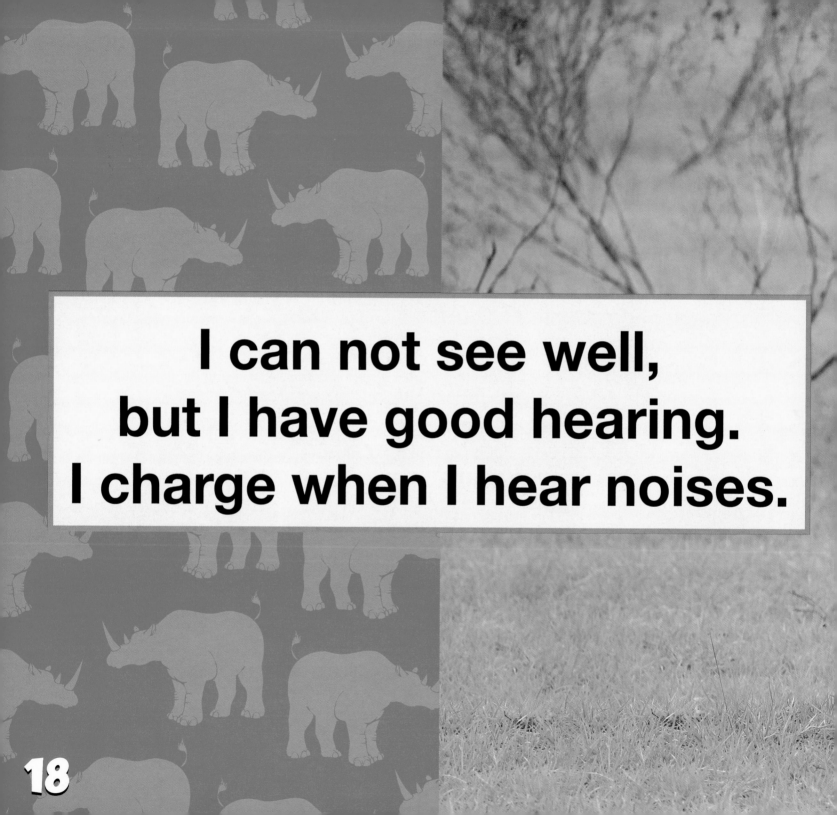

I can not see well,
but I have good hearing.
I charge when I hear noises.

18

I have a large horn on my nose.

I am a rhino.

RHINO FACTS

These pages provide detailed information that expands on the interesting facts found in the book. They are intended to be used by adults as a learning support to help young readers round out their knowledge of each amazing animal featured in the *I Am* series.

Pages 4–5

I am a rhino. There are five species of rhinoceros, or rhino. The black rhino and the white rhino are native to Africa, while the Sumatran rhino, greater Indian rhino, and Javan rhino are all found in Asia. Rhinos have lived on Earth for more than 50 million years.

Pages 6–7

I am the second largest animal that lives on land. The white rhino is the second largest land animal. It can stand up to 6 feet (1.8 meters) tall at the shoulder and weigh up to 7,920 pounds (3,600 kilograms). White rhinos have two horns. The front horn can grow to 5 feet (152 centimeters) in length.

Pages 8–9

I can run 40 miles an hour. The black rhino can run up to 40 miles (64 kilometers) per hour. Rhinos are known for their tendency to charge when they feel threatened. Though rhinos are usually solitary animals, they sometimes gather into small groups. A group of rhinos is called a crash.

Pages 10–11

I only eat plants. Rhinos are herbivores. White rhinos are grazers. They mostly eat grass. Black rhinos are browsers, which means they eat from tree shrubs. They have pointed upper lips that help them grasp tree branches and fruit. The white rhino has a square lip that helps it eat grasses.

Pages 12–13

I weighed almost 150 pounds when I was born.
Mothers give birth to a single calf. The calf weighs up to 150 pounds (68 kg) at birth. Within two hours of birth, the calf will start to walk. It will follow its mother for the first two to four years of its life. The calf drinks its mother's milk during this time.

Pages 14–15

I stayed with my mother for four years.
Between two and seven years of age, the calf will go off to live on its own. It is often forced to leave when its mother gives birth to another calf. By age three, the calf is almost as big as its mother. Rhinos are usually fully grown after seven years.

Pages 16–17

I roll in the mud to take a bath.
Rhinos have very thick skin. Their skin is like armor. It can be up to 0.5 inches (1.3 cm) thick. To keep cool in the heat, and for protection from flies and parasites, rhinos take mud or dust baths. They roll in the mud to cover their entire bodies.

Pages 18–19

I cannot see well, but I have good hearing.
Rhinos cannot see well past about 100 feet (30 meters). They have excellent senses of hearing and smell. They can turn their large ears in the direction of a sound. A rhino's nasal passages take up more space in its skull than its brain.

Pages 20–21

I have a large horn on my nose.
All five species of rhino are endangered. Scientists estimate that the combined total population of all rhino species is about 25,000. The biggest threat to the rhino's survival is humans. Poachers hunt and kill rhinos for their horns.

KEY WORDS

Research has shown that as much as 65 percent of all written material published in English is made up of 300 words. These 300 words cannot be taught using pictures or learned by sounding them out. They must be recognized by sight. This book contains 46 common sight words to help young readers improve their reading fluency and comprehension. This book also teaches young readers several important content words, such as proper nouns. These words are paired with pictures to aid in learning and improve understanding.

Page	Sight Words First Appearance
5	a, am, I
6	animal, is, land, lives, on, only, second, that, the
8	an, can, miles, run
10	have, helps, eat, food, me, plants, up
12	almost, was, when
14	after, for, four, live, mother, my, own, to, went, with, years
16	in, take
18	but, good, not, see, well
20	large

Page	Content Words First Appearance
5	rhino
6	elephant
8	hour
10	lip
12	born, pounds
16	bath, mud
18	noises
20	horn, nose